This book is for everyone who made it possible. Maybe you are sitting there saying, "Did I? Did I have even the smallest hand in helping this book to be born?" Then, dear person, this is for you. And thank you.

———————————

"Let everything happen to you
Beauty and terror
Just keep going
No feeling is final"
— Rainer Maria Rilke

All works in this book are original and belong, technically, to Kalyn RoseAnne. She wanted to share them with you, though, so please be kind and respectful about that. Any and all ripping-off of these poems and essays is highly discouraged. (Plus, they are copyrighted.)

Layout and design: Kimberly Perry
kimberlymariedesign.com

Poems and Essays in Order of Appearance:

Poison Needles in a Paper Cup	5
Holy Week and Missing Ribs	6
What the Textbooks Wouldn't Say	8
Alone, Not Lonely	10
Dayenu	12
White Sugar and Conspiracies	13
Six Degrees of Separation	14
High Wire Darlings	15
Golden	16
For Anne	17
Blood	18
A Warning About Uninhabited Land	19
Definitions of Insanity	21
Abstract Paintings	22
So What	23
Confession	24
Shades of Red	26
Unread Headlines	27
But I am Wild	29
Things I Would Like to Tell You but Probably Won't (At least, not for a very long time.)	30
Two Become One	32
Turquoise Bicycles	33
How Would I Raise a Daughter?	35
Irromantic	37
A Tin Mug and Some Words	39
Deeper than Concrete	41
This Skin is Home (Sometimes You're 23)	43
Instead of Dying	44
On Trying to Write When You'd Rather Just Sleep	45
Ten True Things	46

Poison Needles in a Paper Cup

Maybe the things that brought us here are the things that will wash us away.

Choking on sand and salt and cuffed with seaweed, you tried to swim back out and only succeeded at being swallowed in the vast and dark of the waves.

And he and she, they sat on the shore with their poison needles in a paper cup and their fingernail cuts and laughter and watched the children swim and swim and all the while screaming, "Do not get taken by the waves."

And in one hundred years an old man will sit and think about the sea and somewhere deep inside there is a piece of him that will swim away. And his children will find him on her side of the bed with heart still and the stain of saltwater around his eyes and seaweed cradling his wrists.

And once the mourning has passed, they will take their children to the beach.

Holy Week and Missing Ribs

I sat in the bathtub for twelve days
trying to wash away all the ways I
have been a whore, a liar, a thief
My body became wrinkled and I thought
I had become clean but in the creases
of my pruney skin I found all of the same
dirt I was trying to wash away

That night as I was lying in bed I whispered
every offense I'd ever committed into my pillow
thinking that maybe I could exhale them and
wake as something purer than who I was
when I fell asleep

And when I woke to find them on my pillowcase
waiting to envelope me all over again
I reached for a pen and marked the landscape
of my skin with "Innocent"
And upon looking in the mirror found only smudged ink
My interior and exterior finally aligning

I started crying tears that flowed into the ink
and began to forge trails of clean down my face
I let them come
Tears and tears and tears
until my body was finally clean and I had learned
that I cannot shed the things I've done like snake skin

But instead I should let them die
like vines in a garden still alive
new ones grow wrapping themselves around the decay
as the gardener steps into this chaos and says
"How much more vibrant is the green
when laid next to the brown"

I don't want you to become some faded version
of someone in Cinderella's story
A rib cage with one bone missing
going throughout all the land
trying to find the one that will fit

I don't want that any more than I want
to be the rib bone spending time held to
the chests of men who will end up believing
that I do not fit perfectly

I wanted it to be enough that when
I lay down beside you and you draped
your arm across my waist
we both found enough comfort and peace
to fall asleep

What the Textbooks Wouldn't Say

There are quiet nights spent
calling up our demons and asking
that they forget our names
we were just kids, after all
and dammit
we were trying

That's the thing about being young
we are textbook pages
of trial and error
falling down and getting up
not by way of standing and
brushing off our jeans
but by laying where we fell
until we are high enough to forget

It starts when we are very naive
standing on a mountain top
offering our heart to the world
thinking it is in safe hands
and by the time it gets returned to us
it is bruised and calloused and seems
oddly hollow

With furrowed brow
we place it back in its case
and pull the covers over our heads
because jobs can wait
and school can go fuck itself
and the sun can stop trying to tell
us when we need to rise
Hearts do not obey the sun

But I am going to tell you
two things that the textbooks
wouldn't say

ONE
The weight of our sadness should be felt
until we've tasted every drop
and then we must put the cup back on
the nightstand and throw the covers off

of our faces walking outside into
the wind or the sun or the rain
or whatever is there to greet us
because that is life
and we have an ability to pull air into our lungs
and scream and feel and run
and we'll never do it so long as we
stay in bed

TWO
Even if it's nothing but a ghost train
something heard and not yet seen
listen to the whistle before you feel it
shake the ground
and let yourself be in love with the fact
that you can still fall in love

Alone, Not Lonely
(For Hannah)

I've been home for days but only now am I
brushing New York's tangles from my hair
The city is young in a way that I had only tasted
Staying up with the moon, waiting on the sun to rise
And when she does, we put our hands on our hips (in jest)
and ask where our baby girl has been all night
Cigarettes, dancing, and an endless stream of coffee
Hardly any moments passing without
a mug or a to-go cup in hand

It's easy to forget that time is not
standing still outside of these days

We leave the comforts of home to
expose our skin a little
to what we may find "out there"
"Small world," people say
But people like simple ways to sum up
mysteries like six degrees of separation
And the world is anything but small

So, leave home. Plant your feet in
soil that you only recently learned existed
I'm not sure that flowers grow better in new soil
but let's pretend they do
When you leave, pack your bag
and put no people in it
You will go it alone this time

"But won't I be lonely?" you ask
But lonely and alone are so very different
Alone: You may explore and feel and kiss
this new soil. You will be free to roam. To wander.
To change. To become. To learn. To love everything
that it means to be alone yet not lonely.
Lonely: Remember that even "Max
the king of all the Wild Things
was lonely and wanted to be
where someone loved him
best of all"*

Because we all get lonely
And this is okay
It only lasts if we let it

I'm not sure that I believe you can
never learn to be with other people
if you never learn to be alone
so much as I believe that if you
constantly surround yourself with people
you will never learn the value of solitude

So, pack your bags
But put no people in them
And walk, unencumbered, into this piece of your life

*-Maurice Sendak, Where The Wild Things Are

Dayenu

The Jewish people have a word that they use in song during the Passover
Dayenu, meaning, "It would have been enough"
There is a certain grace in this word as the people who whisper it
choose gratitude instead of want
And in my own prayers I wish to echo this same cry of content

But I have something of a catch-22 of a heart
In my prayers to God I may utter "Dayenu"
Yet when it comes to you I will forever be searching
for a word that means "It could never be enough"

I already have four oceans to remind me of your eyes
And if I were able to bottle your voice and gently uncap it
each night as I drifted into sleep, I'd still want your arms around me
I have kept all of your letters but reading myself in and out of days
just makes me wish you'd write one more
And if one day you'd promise me the rest of your days
I'd ask if you'd still walk with me after

Dayenu. It would have been enough
to wake me with breath in my lungs

But dear. You could come back and promise me ten kisses every day
and I would ask for more

White Sugar and Conspiracies

I was born in the same place in which I was conceived
A bed somewhere in the middle of California
into terms that no one really understood

Raised on conspiracy theories and health food
"Don't trust the government
and try your damnedest not to eat white sugar."

I don't remember what if felt like the first time that I cried
No one does
But I almost wish that I could

In this time and this place I had my first kiss
On this day I was doing this when I got that scar on my right knee
It was in that house that my sister told me
to close my eyes and open my mouth
And it took me at least ten years to give sushi another chance

Then I could say:
It was in that room where I first cried
the one where I was made
It felt like your lungs when you dive into icy water
weight
And the fear that strikes when you're five years old
standing in a department store, and you look up
and the hand you're reaching for doesn't belong your mother

I'm tired of entwining myself with expiration dates
I'm tired of stagnant, shallow water
I'm tired of standing in front of the mirror
and seeing a little girl playing with makeup
unsure of how it's really to be put on

I'll never be able to remember the first time that I cried
And actually
I'll never remember the last

Six Degrees of Separation

One
day I'm sure I will cease to feel as I do now, though at least
Two
times a day I still find myself looking over my shoulder yet again to see if your ghost is there.
Three
months ago I doubt I'd have guessed the things I'd do in an effort to regain my own thoughts. To heal. Now there are
Four
people who have been some form of closer to me than the rest of the world, and somehow the sum of my emotions over this refuses to equate to anything more than an overall indifference. According to your psychology, the fact that my dad left us when I was
Five
will affect me for the rest of my life. It will shade every hint of a relationship I may have with any boy who I look at with affection in my eyes.
Six
degrees of separation.
I will always struggle to not somehow be woven into you.

High Wire Darlings

I don't know how I loved you so fast, or why
I think it is because you are human like the rest of us
I think it is because you are beautiful but you are dying
And I wish that I could be the one to save you
It's going to be my fatal flaw
dying to save everyone
I don't know how it happened that when I saw you high up on that wire
I wanted to throw my arms around you and whisper to you
that you would be okay
you just had to try
I wanted to call you "Baby" though we'd only just met.
And though I despise it as a term of endearment
It fit.
I would have given heavy things to be able to kiss your forehead
tell you how beautiful you are
and have you believe me

And when you asked to kiss me,
I was okay to just be in that moment with you
Before you climbed back up; before I came down
Our lips parted and met in the middle
I wanted to keep you there
locked at some idea of normal
I would have kissed you all night
if it would have saved your life
This time our lips parted ways
and I felt the mystery of losing something
that was never mine
I left you sitting at the table
so eager to get back up
that you hardly cared to see me go
And I understood that I would never call you "Baby"
I understood that your blindness weakness selfishness
would not let you believe in your beauty
or the cleanliness you deserve
I returned home where I fell to the floor in sobs
as the mystery settled into my bones and I began to miss
that which I never knew

I will always wish to save you
But I will never play the part of your heroin
Because even you know that you must be the hero
that saves yourself.

Golden

I think your hands were made of clover leaves
Or maybe you held a whole field in your hand
But I couldn't tell and it couldn't matter
And I couldn't speak
The words that drifted up my throat found the arctic
And it froze them then and there

You were my husband, I said.
You were my children's father, I said.
Your arms were supposed to be around me until I got very, very old, I said
Until my hair was white like the petals on the popcorn trees

Did you know that I met an angel once?
Yes, well, I did
And as he sat at the foot of my bed he asked me to quiet down
I am sleeping, I told him. Don't you know that you entered my world through a dream?
Thoughts are not masked by sleep, he replied
Nor are fears, nor are worries, nor are the fractures placed upon our hearts
And now you must quiet down.

When I woke, I walked beneath the evergreens
And I spoke everything

I wanted to tell you how very sorry I am
about how I tried to cover you in gold

For Anne

I have reached the point of exhaustion in which I am setting out to sea
closing my eyes and letting the rocking of the waves be my lullaby
drift off
drift off
drift off
they lap

I can picture Anne of Green Gables
romanticizing death as she crossed her arms over her chest
allowing herself to be pushed into the calm of the lake
Would the scene have retained its beauty if she had actually drowned?
Suddenly death would have been seen in all its treachery
Would we have had to apologize for trying to romanticize the truth?

Blood

I have four hearts inside of my chest

One is always beating over fragility
and how easy it is to die
It does not beat fast as though it is anxious, afraid
or running from anything
It is a steady drum
Always thinking
about how every minute
we both are in
could be our last

I have a heart that beats in two worlds
the tangible and the supernatural
always depending on where my mind is focused
I wake from nightmares with it racing
and pray in order to calm it and fall back to sleep
It only believes in light because it knows the dark
And once daylight returns
believes, again, that it can save itself

I have a heart of flesh and a heart of thorns
And this is exactly as it sounds
The flesh is weak and it is soft
And it bares itself shamelessly to the world
because this is what it means to be alive
To live in moments that pass without letting them
slip by unnoticed

And the thorns
They are incidental
They are accidental
I wouldn't ever hurt another on purpose
but we all are thorn-hearted
And we will never love
without that thorn in our flesh

Four hearts. That's an awful lot of blood.

A Warning About Uninhabited Land

I have 27 bug bites on my legs
and I hope you don't mind because
I cannot make them disappear
There is only waiting until my
body heals itself

I have scars that I know will
never lighten
but I don't think it bothers you
It doesn't bother me

Let me tell you what I am:
I am an imperfect collection of assorted pieces
My words don't always exit my mouth the way
that my mind told them to
I hate showering every day, especially in winter
And it's taking me a while to trust again
But don't worry
I already have a plan to fake it until
I see that I really don't have to anymore
If you want to love me you should know
that I am not going to try and tame my mind
I know that it's wild and thinks too much
and can't always succeed in getting my heart to listen
But it's the one I was given and I am going to let it be free
I will cry about things that happen to people I've never met
and I will cry more when I feel lonely
I will cry for my friends when they are happy and sometimes
I might even be so happy in my own right that I will cry
Basically, loving me might require a lot of tissues
But don't worry
I don't expect you to always know what to say
or even to say anything
I'll just want to know you're there
You should know that I probably can't make my heart
any tougher than that
When the world told me to grow thistles around it
I just formed bruises
They are very tender but don't worry
They are healing
If you want to love me you should know that I am not
going to build walls around my heart to keep the pain out
It's the one I was given and I am going to let it be free

Let me tell you what I will never be:
I will not be a shallow investment
And I will not invest in shallow ways
Humans were not made out of molds
and I am no exception
So please do not be surprised
if I am asked to fit one and I
tell it to go to hell
I will never fold neatly into compartments
I am not someone that can be tucked away
when that is what's most convenient
I might not really be "convenient"
Unless, to you, convenience looks like
not hiding from rainstorms
because I will never do that
I won't say that I'll never wear sunscreen
Though I hate it
But I will say this
I will never be a vase of flowers
Pretty and quiet
never asking for what they need
yet existing only for your pleasure
and wilting as you pass by them 27 times a day
yet only see them once

Loving me (or any other honest human)
will not be easy or convenient
So, if you plan to love me
you should know
It will require walking without apprehension
into a land that is not so inhabited anymore
(People live there but they have acres between their houses)
Where we love in spite of its difficulty
Well past the point of convenience
Where homes grow up out of ashes
And lovers weather all things together
for the sake of the beloved
for the sake of love itself
and for the fact that it will be worth it
because

in the end
it always is

Definitions of Insanity

It's 85 degrees in the mouth of a man who
will wake up in the morning to find his arms empty
his lover gone
Only 13.6 degrees from normal but enough
to make him feel that he might never be warm again

He's been defining insanity for years
Pouring hot coffee into a cold ceramic tumbler
every day
Always frustrated at how quickly it becomes lukewarm
Never thinking to immerse the container in hot water

In the same way that the one he called "Love"
defined insanity by repetitively opening the fridge
knowing there wasn't anything new to be found
and by expecting her silence to form him into
everything she, herself, wanted to become

What a horrible thing to be called by a name
whose shoes you will never fill
What a beautiful thing to be called by a name
that he already understood no one ever really warrants
but everyone deserves

Abstract Paintings

There are mornings in which you wake
with the whole world sitting on your chest
Wishing that the nausea induced by grief
could rid you of your sadness
The emotion would leave with the vomit
and you could flush it all away

There are two types of pain, I think
I've heard it said that it all hurts the same
"Pain is pain"
But I am stubborn and I might beg to differ
I see the pain of a dagger driven in by another
And I see the pain of being the driver
Stepping back and seeing the pool of blood you've made
Running frantic trying to find anything at all
with which to bind the wound
But you both are naked in a sea of concrete
You finally quit looking for rags
and lay your body over the wound
praying your skin will slow the bleeding
And instead the blood just covers you
Your own wounds bleeding out
add to the painting that a helicopter pilot might
see from above
Abstract. Red and stark white and greyish black
all running together gracefully
But you are on the ground seeing the entanglement
of bodies feeling the cold, unyielding pavement beneath you
without the strength or the tools to send up a smoke signal
"Help. We are not an abstract painting.
We were two lovers caught with knives and
ill-trained hands."

She has come with rags
And really you should go
We won't both be saved at once
And I promise to make it out alive

I am as a bird that has been set down in the
vast and beautiful wild
with freshly clipped wings
Only able to look at the mountains
Unable to soar above them

So What

And so what if everything I read reminds me of you
simply because I know that we are moved in the same ways?

And so what if sometimes poetry, to me, feels like
typing feelings with my eyes closed?

Everything is connected, as I see it
Except my thoughts on many occasions
And they are disconnected much of the time

So what if I fall and bleed
and so what if I fly?
It's not that nothing matters
so much as maybe everything does
or the culmination of everything does

So what if yesterday I stayed in bed
but today I laughed and danced
and felt happy to lay on my back
and watch the stars?

So what if tomorrow I don't want to write
one line?
I wanted to write today.

So what if I'm lonely and yet
find myself
wanting to be alone?

So what? So what? So what.

Confession

I sat down to write a poem about you
and almost immediately stopped wanting to
So, here is the birth story of the first
(and maybe only) poem that I will
write about you:
I don't want to write it

I don't want to read the sadness
that lies both in and in-between the lines
Though I barely know you
I have let you unearth me
Not only do I not know how it happened
but I don't know what to do about it from here

We are not safe people for each other, you and I
I will tell you the whole story of us before you realize
that I have even thought that far ahead

It begins when we are trying to heal from other things
failing in our attempts to act like we have not been
completely charmed by each other too soon
We would whisper I-love-you's into each other's ears
because we liked the way it felt rolling off of our tongues
We might even think we meant it
while we sat outside in the cool night air
laughing and carrying on
as if nothing else mattered but that moment

But I would not be ready for you
And you would not be healed from
having just departed from the person
you've loved for some time
At the end of it, we'd realize
that band-aids just get blood on them

These are the things I tell myself
as a means of protection
hoping to convince myself to stay away
from something that can never be seen
in daylight
I wonder if you have things that
you, also, have to tell yourself to keep away from me

I think it's interesting that this is the second time
that I have written this poem
The first time, I lost the document
that contained it and many others
but this is the only one I couldn't recover

Shades of Red

Silence precedes me in shades of red
A carpet rolled out
The blood of a sacrifice
or of the self-inflicted wounds
we promised never to perform again

But I am speaking all the time
In my use of words and in that same silence
In my waking and my lying down

Because every piece of written and
spoken language
begins in thought

And I tell you, dear
I can't shut up

Unread Headlines

Death rode gallantly in on his high-horse
arrogant in his claim that you were his to take
There I sat, foolishly writhing on the floor
begging that he leave empty handed
He laughed coldly as he carried you away from me

I cross another day off the calendar and I silently whisper
"From here, what?"
Every day during week one I wake with needles
covering the landscape of my skin and I cannot move
I can only lie there as my tears roll away from me
I tried sleeping harder, thinking eventually I'd wake
from a dream, needle-less
and walk down the hall into the kitchen to see you
at the breakfast table
The first time I saw your empty chair I went back to bed
and rolled over. The needles would stay for a while.

It's been thirty days and I still inhale sharply every time
I open the front door and see that no one has brought the paper in
I put it in front of your chair on the table
just in case
I eat only what I can stomach and go to work
You'd be surprised at how numb my body became that first week
I had no choice
I perform my job in a series of disconnected, memorized motions
I act more than I think as feeling is most often a side effect of thinking
But at the end of most days emotion usually washes over me
as the tide might
And I bury my tears in the drops of the shower
and hide my heaving sobs in the blanket you bought for me because
you know that I am always cold
Knew. Dammit, I don't know if I'll ever get used to the past tense

Six months have passed and I canceled the paper just yesterday
I never read it anyway, and it just felt like I was having
daily reminders delivered to the front door
"Good morning. This will sit in front of an empty chair.
No one will open it to find that the loved ones of at least
sixty people in Syria will wake with needles tomorrow.
The ghost you carry inside will never again perform

such human tasks. Will never put its arms around you.
Will never sing you to sleep."
Everyone is insisting that I must "get out of the house more often"
"It's not good for you to be alone so much"
"Come to dinner. We miss you."
I want to scream at them. SHUT UP
WHAT DO YOU KNOW ABOUT MISSING SOMEONE?
But they probably do know and I can't diminish anyone else's
pain just because mine is more current
I go to dinners. I fake smiles. I still feel guilt every time I catch myself
laughing; forgetting that you are gone

The weather is warm again. Just as it was the day you left
Summer was always my favorite but I knew that when
it came again it would be bittersweet
A haunting reminder has made its home in the season
I loved best
Saturday, and I don't have to go to work
I walk quietly but boldly past the place that the paper used to lie
Bringing your blanket outside and spreading it in the sun
It makes me feel like you aren't so far away
The barrier between life and death may be impenetrable
but it is still fluid
A catch-22, I know
You are alive because I keep you alive
Because I can finally look at your picture and smile
Because wrapping in this blanket has become comfort over pain
Because I refuse to take what is left of you and store it away
in a box under my bed
Because I refuse to let the memory of you collect dust
I am sitting in the shade of our favorite tree reading Lord Byron
"The heart will break, but broken live on"

But I Am Wild

Is it so wild to want a revolution of self?
Because this is what I feel underneath my skin
Like smoldering embers ready
to burst into flame

Old self, new self
False self, true self

We shed our skins as we grow older

I feel movement
I feel a resistance to those
who are resistant
to truth
beauty
life-as-art

Cynics
Naysayers

Show me your empire, you who tell me
that I cannot have my dreams
Everything is moving towards art
don't you see?

If standing on top of a building screaming
"LET'S DO EVERYTHING"
Isn't art
Then dammit
I don't know what is

Things I Would Like to Tell You but Probably Won't (At least, not for a very long time.)

I wish that it were easier for me to explain that
you won't really get inside my head for a long time
even though I want you to crawl inside my mind
as badly as I want to curl up with a flashlight
inside of yours and read for hours on end

It's not a rare occasion for me to find myself
behind my thoughts as if they were one-way glass
and my words were on the other side watching them

It's just hard to interrupt a peaceful silence with
"Honestly, I have serious internal conflict about
almost every decision I make these days and
I am not really very happy with how stagnant
things feel right now" when you just learned my favorite
color and we haven't yet memorized how the other one
takes their coffee

Laying on my back, I'll stare at the ceiling
almost blankly except for the one wrinkle
you may find on my almost invisibly furrowed brow
if you look closely enough

You think I'm just quiet. And I am.
But mostly because it's hard to say
"Good morning, if I stay in this town for
another complete year I will probably go
insane" or "This food is delicious but
I am more so wondering if I am pissing away
all my chances to do anything that will
matter once I am dead."

I am too shy to tell you that on many days
I feel the weight of the world as a physical
ache in my chest and that I often wonder
if the right thing to do is give it all up
and live without regard for money
or comfort or any other ideas we get
fed on platters when we grow up
with a grocery store on every corner

Maybe you would like to know how lonely
I feel when I am unknown
but I am still learning to open my mouth
to speak at all the right paces
so that I don't say too much too soon
and I don't stay so quiet that you think my head
is only a graveyard for once-good-thoughts

By the time I tell you everything, it will be too late
We'll be attached in some way
and our makeshift union will have to choose
between solidarity and separation

Two Become One

Every person you will ever
come into contact with
as well as every person whose life you
are aware of only as
the scientific fact that there are now
7 billion of us [walking around,
breathing, hearts beating, minds turning
thoughts over and over like pebbles
in a hand, dying every day]
began as two individuals
in a synchronized time
and none of the said population
can begin as any less than that

Yet, strangely, we are born into
a presupposition that
unless we choose otherwise
we ultimately come to our end alone

Back then I was too young to understand
but I now believe my life
to have begun in its fullest sense
when we took our two realities
and made them one
I hadn't felt safe enough be born
until I had found my home with you
And then like a fawn I found my shaky legs
and learned to walk for the first time
But I stayed young for too long and would
never run beside you
and you patiently walked with me until
you felt like it was to no avail
and we were separated in the woods

In this way, my life now follows the great
mystery of human existence
I began as two
And now I am dying as one

Turquoise Bicycles

I used to have such a handle on
my dependency upon coffee
but something changed on the
day it became the only thing
my body would accept for breakfast

One vice for another,
I suppose. And I know I am not
a smoker as I have taken to calling
my worst a "two cigarette day"
So coffee it is

I don't know how I coped at eight years old
I think it may have been by riding my bike
Which makes me feel a certain
sadness about the way things change
as we grow up and coffee and cigarettes
replace purple and turquoise bicycles

It's a little humorous (though it's not funny at all)
how my reason for sadness is the same
It's something we all go through
at eight years old and again in our twenties
or teens or thirties because pain is a universal experience
It's that talk your parents have with you when
you're moving away from the only best friend
you've known
They say, "Honey, don't cry. You're going
to meet a new best friend."
But your small world view can't
get over the fact that you won't
finish growing up with the first one

I'm not bitter, and I don't think I'm a cynic
Yet still I have somehow become exactly
who I never wanted to be
That girl with worlds of melancholia behind her eyes
who will take a lot of convincing
to finally believe
that there is real love
after first love

(People say, "There are other fish in the sea."
I say, "Fuck you. She was my sea."
-James Faulkner)

How Would I Raise a Daughter?

Warm winter light illuminates the room on this cold Wednesday
the glass panes filtering out any frigidness that looms outside
I'm watching a baby this afternoon
She's 11 months old
She's sick
Seems like most kids are this time of year

When I pick her up out of her crib she turns into my chest
and immediately falls back to sleep
So I sit down in her room, I rock her, I wonder if I will ever decide
to have children
I wonder about raising a daughter

She's going to ask me if Santa Claus exists, you know
And when she does I am going to tell her about time
That once-upon-forever-ago such a word did not yet exist
yet through the ages people came to believe in it firmly
and it is up to her if she wants to believe in either

She's going to ask me about dragons
and I will tell her that no one really knows for sure
but that when something is real to your imagination
it becomes as real as anything else

She's going to come to me asking about broken hearts
and I'm going to ask her to recall what I told her about dragons
And also about her father and how he is the reason
I can tell her it really all becomes what it should eventually

I look at this little girl in my arms and am in awe
She doesn't know anything can hurt her
She doesn't know the pain of not having her needs met
She knows love and warmth and protection
And I wonder how I could ever raise a daughter

How could I possibly teach her about everything?
And then I realize that I can't
I can teach her a handful of truths that she can remember
as she grows
Things she'll think of when I cannot hold her hand anymore
From me she will learn unconditional love

what it is like to accept it and how to give it
In our home, she will learn what self-worth is
And probably how to play music and a little French too
She'll have an understanding that the world
has a desire to take and take and take
And that she must cultivate a delicate balance of
saying no and the beautiful desire to give
She will learn that having a will and an opinion is not
something to be ashamed of
And that her body is her own and she must know that this
doesn't just mean she decides when to give it to another
but also that she must learn to care for it as the strong
and delicate vessel of life that it is

She'll know that dogs are my favorite animal
but that I'm never going to force her to feel the same
And I'll approach many things this way

I will teach her that honesty in all things
even when it is painful and difficult
is always better

I want her to know that as much as the world is daunting
and cruel in its selfishness
it is also bursting with possibility and beauty and goodness

I will only have a daughter if I feel confident
that I can raise her to be a soft white light
against the darkness that will try and close in around her
especially once my own has gone out

Irromantic

Please don't think me bitter
or label this as cynicism
I believe that love is real
and I'll even call it good
I'll even say that it can be
our world made over with
everything beautiful when
we fall into it and it is as it should be

But my skin has started crawling a bit
at the thought of things I'd label romance
and I simply do not want them

Do not fawn over me
You could buy me flowers
but I'd rather you give me
poetry and fiction and decorate
my room with words instead of roses

If there is a song that recalls to memory
the thought of me then please tell me
when we are drunk on wine
and dancing to it in my living room
But give me a mixtape of sentimental things
and I will feel like we are swimming
in a poisonous eternal youth

If you write about me
please wait such a very long time
Be as good as Pablo Neruda and don't make me
sit there while you read it out loud

I don't want you to wear outfits
that were carefully put together
and play every folk song that I've ever loved
because I won't believe you
I'd prefer for you to be everything I need
and not much of what I was expecting
or spent my early twenties wanting

If you write cliches on the internet and
attach my name to them I will be queasy

Do not dote on me
Do not say anything about my eyes
when we are watching the stars

I will know you adore me
by the way you remove the space between us
before we fall asleep
It will be in your eyes even when
you didn't mean to tell me
It will be in your voice just telling me about your day
You can know that I adore you in the same ways
and also when I have seen your worst and still not left

I don't want a love littered with rose petals on beds
and other nauseatingly typical acts of romance
Love is romantic enough and

I will know that you adore me when you stay

A Tin Mug and Some Words

You wrote pages for me
songs. letters. poems.
I've kept the box, though on some days
I think I should burn it as a means of letting go
And when I inhale I realize I am not ready
And will I ever be?
That question haunts me more than most

I'm not worried about what I'm going to do with my life
Or how to replace my car when it finally dies
I quit getting anxious about how many books I want to read
and how many photographs I want to take
And whether or not running three times a week is
really enough exercise

I worry about whether or not I will find it in myself
to burn that box. And stop trying to read your writings
Stop being disappointed when I find that they
are no longer about me
I'm scared that no matter the color of his eyes
I will see your blue ones, and blink twice
trying to hide my thoughts from his gaze

I have been falsely cared for by a handful
of selfish people since you
I'm not going to let that happen anymore
Because you taught me that I am worth more
And if I burned all the letters in that box
and replaced them with thank you cards
I still could not thank you enough
For the strength I found looking back
over your selfless love

I bought this blue-speckled tin mug a while back
to take on a backpacking trip into the northern mountains
I swear I drink coffee for sentimental reasons
more than for anything else
And we all agreed we'd want to make coffee at our camp site
I use it at home now and I always think of our trip
when I cried on Mt. Adams, trailing behind where I couldn't be seen
because of those damn letters

I like the sound that the spoon makes against the tin
when I stir in the cream and sugar. (I take a little of both these days.)
And though I can't explain why
there is something in that sound
that lets me know that everything will be okay
no matter what I do with that box
that's still hidden under my bed

Deeper Than Concrete

It is the end of a long summer day in the mountains
I sit here rubbing my eyes and wondering about going north
New York.
Even my skin is excited, anticipating the freedom that lies
in being away for a time

I grew up in these mountains
the daughter of a single mother
and we moved around too much
to really have roots in one place

First, in a neighborhood where my childhood
tasted of wind hitting my face as I fearlessly
rode my bike down hill
Smelled of the woods, onion grass, and always
watching out for poison ivy
Looked like only coming inside when the
fireflies lit the lawn, often just to get a jar
with holes poked in the lid

After that, on busier streets
apartment complexes
and one time a travel trailer
But it had a rope swing
and a ladder up to the roof
and a girl down the street
who, it seemed, loved few things
more than scaring me with her ghost stories
until I wouldn't stay home alone

But no matter where we were
it wasn't far to the woods
or a stream, if you got brave enough
to wander that deep into the trees
Rope swings, honeysuckle, and
mountains. Always mountains

I say we didn't stay in one place
long enough to really put down roots
and maybe I can't go home to "my old room"
but when I see my mother's face
I am like a tree soaking up rain from the ground
just as I am when I put my feet into
the cool of a riverbed
or pick fresh blueberries from a mountainside
My roots are in the golden hue of the tree leaves
when the light hits them just right
and in the sound of cicadas as I fall asleep
in grass stains on jeans from rolling down hills
and picnics beside the wild flowers
My roots have dug themselves deep into the mountains

and all the splendor of the city
could not uproot me

This Skin is Home (Sometimes You're 23)

    Sometimes you're 23 and standing in the kitchen of your house making breakfast and brewing coffee and listening to music that for some reason is really getting to your heart. You're just standing there thinking about going to work and picking up your dry cleaning. And also more exciting things like books you're reading and trips you plan on taking and relationships that are springing into existence. Or fading from your memory, which is far less exciting. And suddenly you just don't feel at home in your skin or in your house and you just want home but "Mom's" probably wouldn't feel like home anymore either. There used to be the comfort of a number in your phone and ears that listened every day and arms that were never for anyone else. But just to calm you down when you started feeling trapped in a five-minute period where nostalgia is too much and thoughts of this person you are feel foreign. When you realize that you'll never be this young again but this is the first time you've ever been this old. When you can't remember how you got from sixteen to here and all the same feel like sixteen is just as much of a stranger to you now. The song is over. The coffee's done. You're going to breath in and out. You're going to be fine in about five minutes.

Instead of Dying

This morning, I went into the store to get breakfast in last night's clothes. Tired from talking instead of sleeping, kissing instead of talking, holding instead of kissing, and from loving in a non-existent kind of way.

You ask me why I'm sad. I'd like to tell you except that I can't explain the way it washes over me, for a thousand reasons, so many times a day, any more than I can explain how it feels when at every other interval the sunlight falls just right and happiness makes me into its well-loved rag doll again. I can only tell you that I want to know that you sleep better at night when I cling to you like wet clothes. And that one of my favorite feelings is your breath on my back. That when I was a little girl I taught myself not to map out the details of a scenario in the way I wanted it to go because things never happened the way I imagined they would. I can tell you that being alive overwhelms me every hour on the hour and that is sometimes good, sometimes bad, sometimes nothing. Maybe instead of understanding why I'm sad you can know that the first time you put your hands in my hair I was scared of how normal it felt, and I have looked for the same comfort from your hands ever since. It's only my own heartbeat that I cannot stand to feel, but if I can curl up under your arm, beside your ribcage, that precious sound will be louder than my sadness and I will fall asleep just fine.

Tonight, the air smelled of honeysuckles as my bare feet fell on the pavement. I breathed in deeply to remember that I am alive. I poured a cold glass of wine and only looked at it until it adjusted itself to the temperature of the room and wasn't what I wanted anymore, yet I drank it anyway. I filled hours of thoughts I didn't want to have with conversation that I needed as much as I needed bare feet on pavement. This is what I did today instead of dying.

On Trying to Write when You'd Rather Just Sleep

If you keep growing up, there will come a time when you will see a face in a picture that feels as much like home as it does an oddly misshapen memory. One that you can no longer see so much as you can feel. Its details elusive but its outline remaining. A poorly framed snapshot that your grandmother took, not quite in focus, with her thumb partially covering the lens. Yet somehow when you see it you know exactly where you were and what dress you were wearing and that the sky on that Sunday was cloudless. You were just seventeen.

Just because you're some years older doesn't mean that things feel any less pivotal than they did then. And so you fall asleep on your side with your knees bent back and your hands clasped together in a very orthodox fashion. Way too tired to form cohesive thoughts let alone prayers, but your position speaks for itself and internally you are still pleading.

Envisage that you are ten years past this now blurry night. Details will evade you, as well they should. None of us should know the particulars of our lives this far in advance. And without knowing the events that will propel you forward, without an understanding of the reasoning, you know just this: You are okay. In ten years you are okay, and that is how you will find the strength to rise once the sun has yet again kissed the moon goodnight and sent it off to bed.

Ten True Things

I. Earlier, when I needed to feel alive again, I walked up the street to a coffee shop. I thought some combination of fresh air, sun, and the exchange of a five dollar bill for the work of someone's hands would wake me from my hazy daydreams. On the way back to my car, I stepped on a manhole cover and laughed remembering the time that one hadn't been placed on correctly and I almost fell in. Then I remembered that I had been with you when it happened and I fell back to sleep.

II. Growing up feels like your skin no longer fits. Like you just want to crawl out of that thinly stretched space and lay down in the grass and sob for hours. Instead, I am in a cafe eating lunch and trying not to scream. Looking around wondering if anyone else in this building is doing the same thing, wondering if they ever have and, if so, how they got through it. Maybe I would calm down if I just had the assurance that other people have looked in the mirror and no longer recognized themselves. Maybe if I could sit across the table from an elderly woman and have her tell me that she lived through days where the covers over her head felt even better than an embrace and weeks where she drank her tears to keep from wetting her shirt sleeves, but that those years shaped her into an iron skeleton with a tender heart. That "worth it" was an understatement. Maybe then I would feel okay.

III. The most precious part of my day was when a three-year-old little girl reached into her pocket to pull out some time that she then placed gently in my hand. As I put in in my own pocket I said, "Thank you so much." Never in a million years would I tell her the truth about time or how badly I wished our exchange could have been true.

IV. It's said that home is where the heart is, but recent years have me thinking that home is anywhere you have a toothbrush. I think I am down to one.

V. I have spent too many days driving around with a cigarette having had only coffee for breakfast, wearing sunglasses to hide underslept, water stained eyes, and listening to sad songs as if I've discovered some new land that exists only for me. Sadness often feels like the realest emotion, but we must not let it reign over the rest. The weight of sadness is meant to be felt. Lay in it. Let it press down on your chest. Let it shape you. But the minute you start to revel in it, throw it off with great force and walk into a new emotion. Put out your cigarette, finish your coffee, shock your eyes with ice and change the song. Sadness is not to be reveled in.

VI. Poetry makes me want my life to look just like it. I want my eyes to look like poetry. My food to taste like poetry. I want the way I drive a car to be poetic. The way I stretch slowly when I wake up, and the way I lean into the mirror to put poetically red stain on my lips. I want you to see me reading with my back against a tree and my head cocked a little to the side with a gentle expression on my face and think, "She looks so poetic today." I want you to taste poetry when we kiss and God to hear poetry when I tell him secrets. I want my life to look like poetry but I tell myself it's narcissism.

VII. Sit in graveyards. Read the stones and wonder about who lies under them. Gravestones with famous names carved into them mean no more than nameless rocks or bricks left in poverty but just so that loved ones could find them again. In these yards are lovers and mothers. Class clowns and abusive husbands. Teachers and their silent students. Gentlemen who loved their families well. Prostitutes, librarians, and that woman who used to sit in the park and talk to herself. She was a mother, too. People will tell you that one day no one will remember you anymore. Well, maybe one day there won't be a single soul who remembers your name, but maybe their great grandmother does and maybe she taught them how to play piano just like you taught her. Maybe one day the sky will go dark and the world will be ashes floating in space. I cannot pretend to know. I know only that those lovers had lovers and those mothers had children. We are stones cast into the water who simply cannot understand how far out the ripples we create will extend.

VIII. Love will never feel the same way twice. We cannot expect the same set of good things nor should we brace ourselves for the same pains to repeat. We will find new joys. We will create new wounds, and find new ways of healing. Let us not devalue past love, but let us not disgrace love itself by expecting it to look the same way in different light.

IX. It becomes so tempting to say, "Anything is better than nothing." Some days it rings true, but on others "nothing" is a dull and fading ache and "anything" is a little shard of glass. Small, clear, flush with the skin and nearly impossible to remove, becoming a part of you until your body forces it out. Or until your skin heals over it allowing it to stay buried, but present, for always.

X. What I realize I need more than most things is a place that I can fall apart knowing that, by the end of it, the arms that greeted me will be tighter around me. Holding the pieces together. And, when I find it, I will leave a toothbrush.

Kalyn RoseAnne has spent most of her twenty-some years growing up in the mountains.
"Houses are nice," she says, "but once I learned that I could build anything with words I decided to live in them instead." She wishes her eyes were always the shade of blue that they are when she cries but does not wish to cry all the time. She is a human first, a writer always, a photographer sometimes, and many other things most of the time. (Like everyone, right?) Kalyn felt a little weird writing this in third person but not as weird as asking someone else to write it for her.

Made in the USA
Monee, IL
04 December 2022